YOGA IS NOT WHAT YOU THINK IT IS:

A Beginner's Guide

to True Yoga

By

Shikha Narula

**Yoga is not what you think it is:
A Beginner's Guide to True Yoga.**

Copyright © 2019 Shikha Narula

ISBN: 9781086767094

**Published by
Shikha Narula**

This book is Offered
at the Holy Feet of my Guru
Sri Sri Paramahansa Yogananda

Table of Contents

Introduction

In recent decades, yoga, which was originated in ancient India, has spread far and wide. We find yoga studios in almost every city in the world. In the western world, however, yoga has become popular only as a type of fitness system that contains various postures and physical exercises. But true yoga is much more than that!

In this book, I have made an attempt to throw some light on true yoga so that yoga practitioners around the world can enjoy the full benefits that a complete yoga system has to offer.

I have tried to simplify, and present complex concepts of yoga derived from mystical teachings of ancient Indian scriptures and yoga masters in easy-to-understand and simple English.

My intention is to provide a quick reference guide and therefore, I have not delved into too many details. Please consider this as an introductory guide to the deeply mystical yogic teachings. There are several books available online on each topic and you can choose your topic of interest and research further. I have provided an overview of yoga as it is practiced in India.

I hope you will find this book helpful as it will get you started with the right yoga concepts in mind.

Chapter One

What is Yoga?

***

Yoga is not what you think it is. It is not just a set of physical exercises or postures.

Yoga means 'Union with God'.

The goal behind practicing yoga is not just to attain a flexible body but to unite or merge with the Supreme Spirit (in Consciousness).

The ancient sages of India discovered the psycho-physiological methods of uniting the individual consciousness with the Supreme Cosmic

Consciousness of the Spirit. Yoga students or yogis study and practice these methods with the sole goal of uniting with the Spirit (Para Shiva).

"There is but one Self in the lowliest dust and the loftiest Deva. 'Mamamsha', 'My portion', a portion of My Self, says Lord Krishna, are all these Jivatmas, all these living Spirits. For them the universe exists; for them the sun shines, and the waves roll, and the winds blow, and the rain falls, that the Self may know himself as manifested in matter, as embodied in the universe."

The soul is already a part of the Spirit and not separate from it. However, due to the cosmic delusion or Maya, man identifies himself with the limitations of the body and wrongfully imagines himself to be separate from God.

As the sun emanates a million rays, the Spirit emanates the human race. The individual rays may appear to be separate from the sun, but we know that they are a part of the sun. The sun is their source. The rays of the sun radiate and reach the corners of the world, but they are still a part of the sun and merge back into their source at dusk. Similarly, men may appear to have a separate existence, but they are still a part of their

Source, and will merge back into their Source in the end. When the source is forgotten, the rays may appear separate from each other as well. Similarly, men think of themselves as separate from each other. But in reality, we are all one. We are all rays of the same Sun – the Supreme Spirit.

We forget our Source because our awareness is externalized. However, the journey to the soul is an internal one.When awareness is internalized, the Truth is realized.

Man uses 12-14 hours of his day in performing his duties. He is supposed to sleep for 8 hours and use the remaining 2-4 hours in Self-enquiry. But these days, many people are wasting this time in watching T.V. and on social media. Refrain from social media and use that time for meditation, studying the scriptures and chanting. No matter how beautiful our pictures are on social media, the gods are only attracted to devotion.

Seek God First!

"Seek ye first the kingdom of God and His righteousness, and all these things shall be added unto you."

~ Jesus Christ

"Everything else can wait, but your search for God cannot wait. Seek God first!"

~ Paramahansa Yogananda

We are all responsible for our own journey.

"Your own Self-Realization is the biggest service to mankind."

~ Ramana Maharishi

The ultimate goal of life is not to acquire massive wealth, name and fame. All this is temporary and will be left behind at the time of death. The ultimate goal is to realize the Self.

Self-Realization bestows liberation from this worldly cycle of birth and death and therefore, from pain, suffering and misery that only belong to this physical world.

"In God you will tap the Reservoir of perennial, unending Bliss."

~ Paramahansa Yogananda

We keep running after things, thinking that they would make us happy and hoping that that happiness will last forever. But we all know that it does not last long. Then, we set new goals and start running after something else and the cycle continues.

The truth is that we are after that Blissfulness that is our very nature. We are not after anything that's external to us. We are after our own true Self. We feel lost because we have lost touch with our own Self, and we try to cover up for that loss by seeking outside of us because no one has taught us yet to look within. But when we turn within, and seek into the depths of our own being, and discover our true nature, we experience eternal bliss. All desires are fulfilled when the Self is found. We stop running after things. Whatever we need comes to us on its own. We become spiritual magnets.

God, Self, atman(soul), universe, love, peace, bliss, infinity, eternity, pure consciousness – all these words describe THAT one thing only. They are thought to be separate from each other due to ignorance or limited knowledge (avidya). For a Self-Realized being, there is no difference between these terms.

The journey to the Self begins with Self-enquiry. Self-enquiry begins with the question, "Who Am I?"

The truth is that we are neither the body, nor the mind. The body is only a vehicle of the soul, and mind its tool. We are the atman(soul) that sprang out from the Spirit just like a wave emerges from the ocean.

However, we are still floating in the ocean of Spirit. And when we discover our true identity, we merge back into the ocean of cosmic consciousness just as the wave merges into the ocean after a temporary individual existence.

The soul is encased in three bodies – the causal body, the astral body (subtle) and the physical body (gross). As the soul's consciousness descends from causal to astral and from astral to physical, it accepts the limitations of this gross physical world and therefore, forgets its true nature and loses its powers. However, as a yogi, through self-effort and self-enquiry uses the body (pranayama and meditation) and mind (studying the scriptures) as tools to experience his own nature in its full glory, the veils of Maya (delusion) and avidya (ignorance) are torn apart, and the soul merges with its source.

***

The Supreme Spirit is formless and pervades everything – living and non-living. Man was made in the image of God. Therefore, only man, among all living beings has the capacity to rise up to the level and consciousness of the Supreme Spirit. Its true nature is 'pure consciousness' and it is experienced as peace, bliss, infinity and eternity.

In Hinduism, the Supreme Spirit is called Para Shiva or Para Brahman. 'Para' means 'beyond'. Since the Supreme Spirit is beyond time, space and form, it is called Para Shiva and its energy is called Para Shakti. When the Spirit takes a masculine form, we call Him God and when the Supreme Spirit takes a feminine form, we call Her a Goddess.

The Supreme Spirit performs different roles as different Gods and Goddesses much like we change garments according to different occasions. It takes form as the Trinity – Brahma (the creator), Vishnu (the preserver) and Mahesh (the destroyer or regenerator). Their energies (Shaktis) are called Saraswati, Lakshmi and Parvati respectively. Therefore, these Gods and Goddesses are neither superior nor inferior to each other.

The devout Hindu first chooses any one **form** of God and aims to unite with Him/Her through the practice of Yoga. This type of union is called **Savikalpa Samadhi.**

After experiencing the Savikalpa Samadhi, the yogi continues to strive and finally unites with the **formless** Supreme Spirit – Para Shiva. This type of union is called **Nirvikalpa Samadhi**.

When the yogi experiences Nirvikalpa Samadhi, he/she attains the status of an angel/god in the Higher Realms. The Yogi attains liberation from the cycle of birth and death even though he may still be living in a physical body. When his time here is finished, his soul enters the Highest spiritual/astral plane.

The yogi who has united his consciousness with the Supreme Consciousness does not identify himself with his body or his material possessions. He is free from attachments. His consciousness merges with the universal consciousness and therefore he feels that the entire universe is his body. He feels the love and energy flowing through all form and knows that he is that love and energy. Such a yogi declares, 'I Am That' or 'I Am Shiva'.

Such a yogi is called a **'Self-Realized'** being as he has realized that his Self (atman) is nothing but Para Shiva or Para Brahman. He is a **'Jeevan mukta'** as he is not subject to rebirth and lives in the body only as long as his

Prarabdha Karma is not resolved. When he leaves the body, he is called **'Videha mukta'**.

This, in a nutshell, is the ultimate goal of Yoga.

Chapter Two

What are the four

types of Yoga?

***

"The rousing of the Kundalini is the one and only way to attaining Divine Wisdom and superconscious perception, the realisation of the spirit. It may come in various ways, through love for God, through the mercy of perfected sages, or through the power of the analytic will of the philosopher."

~ Swami Vivekananda

There are different types of people and therefore, there are different types of Yoga.

Some people enjoy physical workouts and have a strong body, while some are devotional and love singing and dancing. Some are too busy trying to find a balance between work and personal life, while some have a sharp intellect and a curious mind and want to understand the mysteries of the universe!

The good news is that Hinduism offers a unique yoga practice for each type. These are broadly classified into four main categories.

The four categories are as follows:

***

Raja Yoga

Raja Yoga is the science of Self-Realization. It is a combination of hatha yoga (physical exercises and postures), pranayama (breathing exercises), and meditation. This type of yoga involves a deep study of the physical body, the astral body (subtle energies, nadis, chakras, and kundalini), as well as the mind (subconscious, conscious and superconscious) E.g. Kriya Yoga, Kundalini Yoga, Ashtanga Yoga, etc.

Hatha Yoga aims to strengthen the body and awaken the dormant Kundalini Shakti that lies at the base of the spine. Meditation requires sitting erect in a chosen form of asana for an extended period. To do this, we need a strong body. Therefore, Raja Yogis practice Hatha yoga first to strengthen their body, especially their back.

Pranayama aims at controlling prana through control of breath. Breath is not prana. Breath is a manifestation of prana. Pranayama includes a set of breathing exercises. It encourages rhythmical breathing. When we breathe rhythmically, it balances and harmonizes the body. Also, when kumbhaka (breath retention) is exercised, it awakens the kundalini.

Scientifically speaking, when breath retention or kumbhaka is practiced, it opens multiple pathways that were earlier dormant. When all these pathways are opened, full brain is activated, thus leading to Superconsciousness.

Prana is the vital force or energy that moves in our body. Prana is the life force. This prana does not move randomly. It flows through energy channels called nadis. In all, there are 72,000 nadis. However, these are not physical nadis. They cannot be seen with the physical eyes. We cannot see our breath. We cannot see the vital force. But it is there. It is what gives us life. It is a part of the astral body or the energy body. These nadis meet at special energy centers called chakras. The seven chakras are : **Muladhara** (the root chakra located at the base of the spine), **Svadhisthana** (the sacral chakra located below the navel), **Manipura** (the navel chakra located at the navel center), **Anahata** (the heart chakra located at the heart center), **Vishuddha** (the throat chakra located at the base of the throat), **Ajna** (the third eye chakra located between the eyebrows), and **Sahasrara** (the crown chakra located just above the crown of the head). Out of the large number of nadis, the most significant ones are

Ida, **Pingala** and **Sushumna**. Ida is on the left and Pingala on the right. Ida begins in the muladhara chakra at the base of the spine and ends in the left nostril while Pingala, though originating from the same location ends in the right nostril. Sushumna is a hollow canal that runs through the center of the spine. At the lower end of Sushumna lies **Kundalini Shakti** coiled up in a triangular form. When, through pranayama and meditation, this kundalini is awakened, it rises up through this hollow passage, step by step or chakra by chakra, finally reaching the Sahasrara (topmost chakra) and thus granting liberation to the yogi as the Kundalini shakti unites with Shiva at the top. This union of Shiva and Shakti is yoga.

There are many books dedicated to each of the above subjects. For those who are interested in the Raja Yoga path, understanding these concepts is crucial. Therefore, I would recommend all Raja Yogis to study these concepts well before beginning their practice and always meditate under the guidance of a Guru. Your Guru may not be living in a body, but he can still guide you from the Higher Realms.

If you enjoy pranayama and meditation, do consider joining the Self-Realization Fellowship (SRF) or Yogoda Satsanga Society (YSS) founded by Sri Sri Paramahansa Yogananda.

If you are a Shiva Devotee, do study Kashmir Shaivism. The book Vijnana Bhairava gives us 112 meditation techniques to realize the Self. However, a good foundation is necessary. Study the Shiva Sutras first. Then explore the other Kashmiri Shaivite scriptures like Spanda Karikas (The Doctrine of Vibration) and Pratya-bhijna-hrydayam. Once you have understood the key concepts, you can practice the techniques given in Vijnana Bhairava.

Many westerners find this study difficult as many terms are in Sanskrit. In that case, you can study the teachings of Saiva Siddhanta as explained by Satguru Sivaya Subramuniyaswami (founder of Kauai's Hindu Monastery) through his Master Course trilogy (Dancing with Siva, Living with Siva and Merging with Siva) first.

I studied the teachings of Saiva Siddhanta, Kashmir Shaivism and SRF/YSS. But there are many more yoga schools/ashrams in India that teach Raja Yoga. Many of these Yoga schools have now established their centers in the west too. You can browse through their websites and choose the one you feel most inclined to.

***

"That love is highest which is concentrated upon God. When such speak of God, their voices stick in their throats, they cry and weep; and it is they who give holy places their holiness; they make good works, good books better, because they are permeated with God. When a man loves God so much, his forefathers rejoice, the gods dance, and the earth gets a Master!"

~ Narada Bhakti Sutras

"The bondage can only fall off through the mercy of God, and that this mercy comes to the pure. So,

purity is the condition for the bestowal of His mercy. How that mercy acts? He reveals himself to the pure heart, and the pure and stainless man sees God."

~ Swami Vivekananda

Bhakti Yoga

A pure heart is a heart full of love, for love is pure and love is God. This is a path of intense love and devotion. A true bhakta loves God relentlessly, selflessly and unconditionally. He loves God for love's sake and not for any rewards. He chants His name, sings His glories and dances in joy. He experiences bliss as he is filled with the nectar of love.

Chanting (Japa Yoga) falls under this category and is a very important part of Bhakti Yoga. The devotee chants the mantra (name) of His chosen form of God (Shiva, Krishna, Devi, Ganesha or any other form). The mantra purifies the body, mind and the environment. It uplifts the spiritual energy of the person and the place where it is being chanted. It creates a protective shield around the devotee and increases his intuitive powers.

Continuous chanting (Japa) leads to **Ajapa** which is the highest form of Japa. This happens only by the grace of God or Guru. When Ajapa begins in the heart, the devotee hears the mantra going on in his heart continuously and effortlessly.

By ceaseless devotional chanting alone, the kundalini shakti which lies at the base of the spine is awakened. As the devotee dances in joy, the kundalini starts dancing too and starts rising through the Sushumna nadi (the central nadi) and reaches the top-most chakra where union of Shiva and Shakti takes place (yoga).

Therefore, the devotee (bhakta) or one practicing bhakti yoga, need not practice Hatha yoga asana, pranayama or meditation (Raja Yoga).

While in Raja Yoga, the yogi himself takes arduous efforts to awaken and uplift the Kundalini Shakti within the center of his spine, in Bhakti Yoga, the Guru or God lifts the devotee to the Highest level of Consciousness through Grace. Therefore, this path is easier to practice.

***

"A man ought to live in this world with his heart for God and his hands for work."

~ Lord Krishna

Karma Yoga

Service to mankind is service to God. This type of Yoga is suitable for the duty-bound individual. It is turning ordinary work into spiritual practice.

This is a path of selfless action (karma) according to dharma (scriptural teachings) without thought of reward. By serving others, the individual cultivates humility, which is the first step towards God. Therefore, in many ashrams in India, this type of yoga is practiced first. The yogi is assigned with many duties in the ashram.

There is only one thing that stands between man and God – the egoistic mind.

Once the ego is subdued, the deeper philosophical truths are then introduced slowly through the practice of Jnana Yoga.

***

"Jnana is knowledge. To know Brahman as one's own Self is Jnana. To say, "I am Brahman, the pure, all-pervading Consciousness, the non-enjoyer, non-doer and silent witness," is Jnana. To behold the one Self everywhere is Jnana."

~ Swami Sivananda

"The things which a man of the world thinks valuable, a Spiritual man must cast aside as worthless. The diamonds of the world, with their glare and glitter in the rays of the outside sun, are mere fragments of broken glass to the man of knowledge. The crown of the King, the scepter of the

Emperor, the triumph of earthly power, are less than nothing to the man who has had one glimpse of the majesty of the Self."

~ Annie Besant

Jnana Yoga

This is a path of divine knowledge or divine wisdom. Therefore, it is also called the 'yoga of wisdom'. It begins with Self-enquiry – Who am I? This type of yoga involves a deep study of the scriptures, contemplating on them and realizing those truths in one's own meditation. Since yoga is an experiential path, mere theoretical knowledge of the scriptures is not enough. *Realization comes through experience.* The Yogi is called a Jnani only after he *realizes* the Truth that the soul(atman) and Brahman (Para Shiva) are one.

All the other modern types of yoga fall under one of these main categories.

The practices involved in each type of yoga differ from each other. Therefore, the spiritual experiences that these yogis have also differ from each other. For example, a Raja yogi's experiences will differ slightly from that of a Jnana Yogi.

Yoga is an experiential path. One may not see or experience much in the beginning. But as the yogi endures and continues with his spiritual practice, he starts experiencing the subtle energies that move in his body and in the universe.

It is advisable that the yogi incorporates all types of Yoga in his daily sadhana (spiritual practice) as it will accelerate his spiritual evolution.

For example, a raja yogi may meditate for four hours a day and spend only an hour in studying the scriptures while a Jnana yogi may study the scriptures for four hours and meditate only for an hour.

It is important to study the scriptures or the teachings of one's Guru as the experiences that one may go through while practicing yoga are explained in the scriptures. It is also said that if a yogi does not understand the meaning of his experiences, then its essence is lost. Therefore, it is necessary that the yogi studies the scriptures.

It is not possible to study all the scriptures. That is not required either. One may choose a path among the many paths that Hinduism offers – Shaivite, Vaishnavite or the Shakta path.

Shaivites are devotees of Lord Shiva. Vaishnavites worship Lord Vishnu and His incarnations like Lord Krishna and Lord Rama. Shaktas worship the Divine Mother.

Each sect has its own literature. The Yogi can choose what to study according to his own inclination.

No matter what type of Yoga one practices, it is always essential that he also practices Bhakti Yoga (the path of Devotion). Without Bhakti (love for God), yoga (union) is impossible.

Study and Practice the Advaita (non-dual) philosophy. The Advaita philosophy emphasizes on the fact that the Self is not separate from Shiva, but is Shiva indeed. In other words, THOU ART THAT.

Yoga (union) does not take time for one who has purified his body and mind. But it takes will power.

Chapter Three

The Twenty Commandments

***

The Saivite scriptures have outlined twenty commandments called 'The Yamas and the Niyamas' that every yogi has to practice before he begins with intense yoga. These are simply do's and don'ts for spiritual living. Yama means 'to restrain'. Therefore, it outlines the don'ts. Niyama means 'to practice or follow'. Therefore, it outlines the dos.

The yamas and niyamas help in purifying the body and mind. Also, Yogis keep their karma in check by

practicing the twenty commandments.

The yamas and niyamas are as
follows:

YAMAS: RESTRAINTS

1. Ahimsa: Noninjury
Do not harm others by thought, word
or deed.

2. Satya: Truthfulness
Refrain from lying and betraying
promises.

3. Asteya: Nonstealing

Neither steal nor covet nor enter into debt.

4. Brahmachariya: Sexual Purity
Control lust by remaining celibate when single and faithful in marriage.

5. Kshama: Patience
Restrain intolerance with people and impatience with circumstances.

6. Dhriti: Steadfastness
Overcome non-perseverance, fear, indecision and changeableness.

7. Daya: Compassion

Conquer callous, cruel and insensitive
feelings toward all beings.

8. Arjava: Honesty
Renounce deception and
wrongdoing.

9. Mitahara: Moderate Appetite
Neither eat too much nor consume
meat, fish, fowl or eggs.

10. Saucha: Purity
Avoid impurity in body, mind and
speech.

NIYAMAS: PRACTICES

1. Santosha: Contentment
Seek joy and serenity in life.

2. Tapaha: Austerity
Perform sadhana, penance, tapas and sacrifice.

3. Dana: Charity
Tithe and give creatively without thought of reward.

4. Astikya: Faith
Believe firmly in God, Gods, guru and the path to enlightenment.

5. Isvarapujana: Worship

Cultivate devotion through daily worship and meditation.

6. Mati: Cognition
Develop a spiritual will and intellect with a guru's guidance.

7. Siddhantasravana: Scriptural Study
Study the teachings and listen to the wise of your lineage.

8. Hri: Remorse
Be modest and show shame for misdeeds.

9. Japa: Recitation

Chant holy mantras daily.

10. Vrata: Sacred Vows

Fulfill religious vows, rules and observances faithfully.

Chapter Four

The Law of Cause and Effect and the three types of Karma

***

Karma is the universal law of cause and effect. Whatever we sow, so shall we reap. However, Karma is not just limited to our actions. Our thoughts, words and deeds together make our karma. Whatever we send out in the universe through our thoughts, words and deeds comes back to us in time through other people. Kind and loving deeds bring loving reactions.

Selfish and hurtful acts bring suffering. Karma is a divine law of justice. It punishes misdeeds and rewards good deeds.

There is also mass karma that affects a group of people, such as a religion, a state or a country. For e.g., droughts or famines affecting a region is a result of mass karma of people inhabiting that region or state.

Human suffering is a result of man's ignorance of the divine law.

Karma is our teacher as it teaches us to refine our behavior. As individuals mature and evolve spiritually, they learn to refrain from misdeeds through understanding.

The Three Types of Karma

There are three types of Karma:

1.Sanchita Karma

This is the sum total of all our past lives' karma.

2. Prarabdha Karma

Prarabdha is that part of sanchita karma which the individual must experience in the present life. In other words, it is the result of previous karmas, that is to be experienced in this life.

3. Kriyamana Karma

Kriyamana is the karma that is currently being created. Some of it will bear fruit in this life, while some will be stored for a future life.

We learn from this Karma theory that it shapes our future. Therefore, we strive to do good in the present so that our future delivers only good events and circumstances and our future life or lives go on smoothly.

One good karma cannot wipe out one bad karma. Good and bad karmas have their individual results.

As long as unresolved karmas lie dormant, reincarnation takes place. Once all karmas are resolved, the soul is liberated from the cycle of birth and death.

Therefore, yogis take karma very seriously. Their constant effort is to take appropriate action to mitigate the effects of previous karmas or wipe them out completely and to create only good karma in the present.

All the practices involved in the four types of yoga wipe out karmas effectively.

Chapter Five

The Mind

***

Before beginning with the practice of yoga, it is essential to understand the nature of the mind. Mind is restlessness itself. It is the mind that stands between man and the Self God within. Therefore, the yogi strives to conquer the mind and put it to rest. All types of yoga directly or indirectly aim to quieten the mind.

The reflection of a full moon is seen in all its glory in a calm lake. Similarly, the reflection of God is seen within as light, when the mind is calm. We can see a glittering mixture of golden and white light in the heart, white light surrounded by blue light in the spiritual eye and a mixture of light colors (transparent light) above the head.

The Pure Consciousness experience (Nirvikalpa Samadhi) is even beyond the light experience.

Mind and breath (prana) are closely associated. In fact, they are directly connected with each other. When the mind is calm, the breathing slows down automatically and vice versa. Therefore, the yogi chooses to either control the mind or the breath, and the other is calmed automatically.

For e.g., the practice of pranayama aims at controlling the breath, so that the mind is automatically controlled. Yes, it does come with several health benefits too. Therefore, practicing pranayama leads to a healthy body and a peaceful mind.

However, in yogic science, prana does not mean breath alone. All the forces and energies of the universe combined are nothing but prana. The different forces are but manifestations of this prana. Therefore, one who has controlled prana can control the forces of nature.

While performing our day-to-day activities, we live in ordinary consciousness. That is the time when our **Conscious Mind** is active. When we go to sleep, we enter subconsciousness. That's when the **Subconscious Mind** is active. And when we enter a peaceful meditative state where we lose consciousness of our body and transcend this ordinary world of forms, we enter Superconsciousness. That's when the **Superconscious Mind** is active.

In meditation, the yogi withdraws his senses thus turning away from the world and ordinary consciousness and enters the subconscious mind. The subconscious mind then opens the gate to the Superconscious mind.

However, most beginners get stuck in the subconscious mind. They find it difficult to go beyond the subconscious. Many fall asleep. This usually happens when the body is tired and needs rest. Many start dreaming in this state.

These dreams should not be confused with visions. Dreams are created by the impressions stored in the subconscious mind. Dreams are 'Subconscious Seeing' while visions are 'Superconscious Seeing'. We forget our dreams within a few hours after waking up. However, we never forget our visions. They stay with us forever. Decades may pass, but we can still see and feel those visions as if they were taking place right before us in that very moment. Sometimes, they may appear a bit hazy after many years pass, but we never forget them and still feel the energy. That is how we can differentiate between dreams and visions.

What is a good meditation experience? My Guru defined meditation as 'concentration on God'. And God is peace. A good meditation experience brings peace. Whenever we feel peaceful after meditation, it means we have touched the Self God within. The deeper we dive, we come out as more peaceful beings with a better understanding of our own Self.

While a Raja yogi strives to attain this peaceful state by practicing pranayama and meditation, the jnana yogi uses the knowledge attained by scriptures and his own mind to enquire into its own nature and thus realizing that the mind, ego and this world are indeed only false appearances that create delusion and separate self from Self or man from God. However, the jnana yogi must realize this truth through experience. Mere theoretical knowledge does not lead to liberation. Due to the Grace of God and Guru, the jnani experiences these truths within himself soon after he has intellectually grasped the Truth. The more devoted he is, the sooner the Grace is received.

While a Raja yogi strives to lift his Kundalini, chakra by chakra; in case of Jnana yogis and Bhakta yogis, it is uplifted by the Grace of God.

The effects can be seen in the body. A yogi's mind is always peaceful as his breathing is slowed down naturally. While an ordinary man completes one breath cycle in 4 seconds, thus breathing 15 times in a minute; a yogi breathes only 1 to 6 times in a minute in ordinary consciousness depending on the activity that he is involved in. He attains the breathless state in meditation. This is true for all yogis. All paths lead to the same goal.

Chapter Six

The Creator and His Creation

***

The Creator of the Universe is Himself uncreated. He is formless and shines in Pure Cosmic Consciousness. He is eternal, self-effulgent, omniscient, omnipresent and omnipotent. Countless worlds emerge from Him as waves arise from the surface of the ocean. These worlds come into being and disappear into Him at the end of the epoch.

When a thought arises in the mind of the creator, manifestation takes place. Therefore, the cosmic mind is the creator of this universe. The entire universe is but His form. These forms appear and disappear, but the Supreme Spirit of the nature of Pure Consciousness Himself remains unchanged.

He creates the universe out of His own essence and thus the entire universe is permeated with Him.

The Creator is the Supreme Intelligence that supports the entire universe. And every thought that arises in this Supreme Intelligence gives rise to form. Thus, the entire manifested universe is only of the nature of thought of the Creator.

He is the eternal and infinite Light in which the universe shines. The

Supreme is Self-luminous. The sun and the moon borrow their light from this Supreme Light.

As this entire universe is contained *in* the Supreme itself, whether manifest or unmanifest, we can say that the Supreme alone exists.

As the Supreme alone exists, there is none other. Therefore, none other can realize the Supreme but Supreme itself.

The entire universe sits in Supreme, and the Supreme sits within the hearts of all sentient beings as light and pure consciousness. He is the life of all. He is the Supreme energy and all the forces too. He is the universe. However, the Universe is not He.

Even as an ornament made of gold is nothing but gold, irrespective of its appearance as a ring, a bracelet or a necklace, the multiple forms of this universe are nothing but the Supreme Intelligent Being Himself.

Just as coldness is inseparable from ice and heat from fire, the world is inseparable from the Creator.

Every creation is a manifestation of the Creator Himself. The Creator is not separate from His Creation. He creates and then fills His creation with His essence. Therefore, nothing exists apart from the Creator. The Creator alone exists.

The Creation is only a reflection of the Cosmic Consciousness of the

Creator. An entire city can be reflected in a small mirror. When we look at the mirror, we see the city. But is the reflected city real? Can the reflection exist without the mirror? Is the reflected city separate from the mirror?

For example, we have thousands of files and folders in our laptop. We use the laptop to browse unlimited websites. There is constant activity. New files are created, old ones are deleted. All this activity is *reflected* on the screen of your laptop. All these files are contained *in* the laptop. They cannot exist outside it. Therefore, we can say that the laptop creates and sustains these files and when the files are deleted, laptop alone remains.

Nothing changes for the laptop. The laptop is aware of every file in its system, but it does not get involved in any of the activities. It gives them the power to function properly, but these powers are limited. And the laptop itself sits and watches everything like a silent witness. For example, when I create a word file, I have my free will to type whatever I want. The laptop does not start typing on its own. It gives me free will to type whatever I want. While we are acting with free will, sometimes, our intuition guides us when we go wrong. Similarly, while we are typing, it may give us autocorrect suggestions. We may accept it or ignore it.

We watch shows and movies on Netflix and YouTube, etc. We get involved in the characters. We laugh and cry with them. But are they real? Isn't it just a show? A play? But how real it seems. So is our world. And what happens when we shut down the laptop. Everything shuts down. The world disappears. There is only peace and calm.

The laptop is like the Supreme Cosmic Consciousness and the individual files are like the individual *jivas* or beings with limited individual consciousness.

(*This is merely an example and should be used only to understand what is explained above and nothing beyond it. The Supreme Consciousness has unlimited powers, and nothing can be compared with it. However, for the sake of explaining its basic functions and how it can be related to individual consciousness, I have used this example.)*

Let's try to understand this with another example. When we look at a beautiful landscape painting, we look at majestic mountains, rivers, trees, birds, houses, children playing and so on. But we forget that it is the canvas, which is in itself attributeless, plain and white (*Absolute Reality*), that holds and sustains the entire painting. Without the canvas, the painting cannot exist. And, the painting is nothing but canvas. When we wash off the paint, the canvas alone remains. Nothing really changes for the canvas. It remains unchanged. The painting was only a temporary manifestation that caused delusion and due to that delusion, we started looking at things separately such as the mountains, trees, rivers, and so on and forgot about the canvas even though the canvas held the painting and was present in every millimeter of the painting. For as long as the painting existed, the canvas though in itself plain and white, accepted the colors painted on it and appeared as that color. We started calling that portion of the canvas as a pink flower, even though it was in truth nothing but the canvas. For as long as the pink flower existed, it was inseparable from the canvas. It could not have existed outside or without the canvas.

The Canvas is like the Unmanifest Absolute Reality, Shiva and the landscape painting is like the manifested universe or Shakti. Shiva and Shakti are One. They are inseparable.

Even as there are multiple rules that are to be followed by the artist while painting (e.g. fat over lean, no acrylics on oil and so on), there are laws of the universe. Now, I know that if I paint ignoring the rules, my oil paints are bound to crack and disrupt the painting. Similarly, if we fail to obey the laws of the universe, disruption takes place.

Now, let's try to have a conversation with some of the birds and trees in the painting.

Imagine that you and I are walking down a beautiful path with trees on both sides. We stop to talk to a tree.

I ask, "Who are you?"

The tree replies, "I'm an apple tree. My name is Appy."

I reply, "Nice to meet you Appy. So, what do you do?

Appy replies, "Oh, I produce apples and provide humans with my fruits and help them stay healthy and strong. That is my duty as an apple tree. I also make abundant good karma by performing my dharma (duty). Here, take some apples for yourself!"

Appy drops two apples for you and me.

"That's great, Appy! Thank you for the apples!" I reply.

Appy just taught us some great stuff. It taught us about Karma, about service without thought of reward, selfless giving and being true to one's nature and performing one's duties.

We continue walking down the path and reach a lovely garden. We enter the garden and find a tiny little bird sitting on a bench.

You ask the bird, "Who are you?"

"My name is Cooki", the bird replies.

"What do you do Cooki?" you ask.

"Oh, I love to sing to the kids that come every morning to play in the garden. They gather around to hear my song and then carry on with their play. Except One!" Cooki stops talking and starts looking around as if searching something or someone.

"Except who, Cooki?" I interrogate.

Cooki sings to us:

*"I know a lovely little girl, a quiet one,
Who comes to the garden every day,*

The kids invite her, but she seems shy,
Oh, I wonder why she doesn't play!"

"Oh! How beautiful and interesting! We would like to meet that girl!" I reply.

"There she comes!" Cooki exclaims.

We walk towards her.

"How peaceful and radiant!" I think.

We shake hands with her and greet her.

"Hello darling, what's your name?" I ask.

"Well, what's in a name? I'm just another you!" she replies.

She walks towards a bench and sits on it.

"Interesting!" We exchange glances.

We follow and sit next to her.

"So, why don't you play with the other kids?" I inquire.

"Because I'm not limited to this little play. I sit here and watch the universe play its thing. I'm only a silent witness." She explains.

"Wow! How old are you?" You ask.

"I don't age at all. I'm ageless. What you are looking at is just a body made of flesh and bones that is subject to age and death. I am Pure Consciousness! And so are you. Sit here with me in this very garden and close your eyes and look within yourself. First, you will see blue light.

Then white light. Enter that channel. Keep going deeper into that tunnel till you reach the end of it. You will reach a state which is beyond light. You will have no form, no body, but you will find yourself everywhere. You will realize that you are infinite and eternal. You will be fully aware. And you will declare too, that you are pure consciousness. The world will disappear. For it never really existed. You alone have been, you alone are and you alone will be. There is none other than you."

I kiss her on the cheek and say, "My little girl, you are *enlightened*!"

Chapter Seven

What is Consciousness?

***

Kashmir Shaivism teaches us that the Highest Reality, the Ultimate and Absolute Truth, the Supreme Spirit is of the nature of Pure Universal Consciousness (Chit) and Universal Psychic Energy or Power (Shakti). Everything that exists in this universe exists within the range of this Consciousness.

It is both transcendent and immanent.

It is the cause of the universe and brings about the manifestation of the universe out of its own free will.

This supreme power is not dependent on any other extraneous material cause.

Chit or Pure Consciousness is all-pervading and eternal. It cannot be restricted or divided by time, space or form. It is non-dual. It is self-luminous, in the light of which the entire universe shines. *Chit* itself flashes forth in the form of innumerable worlds. Therefore, it is not only the cause of the universe but also the effect.

This *Chit* is nothing but the Supreme Lord Shiva Himself. The entire universe is His body. As unmanifest Absolute Reality, He is called Para Shiva. He is immanent and transcendent.

Para Shiva is a mass of Consciousness and Bliss and has absolute freedom to do and know all things (Will, Knowledge and Action).

It is the nature of the Supreme to manifest or create as creativity is its very essence.

Just like a wave emerges from the ocean for a limited time period and then merges back into its source, similarly, everything in this universe emerges from this ocean of Consciousness or Shiva and finally merges back into its source.

The word 'Prakash' means 'Light', but when used to explain consciousness; it does not refer to physical light. Prakash is the light of consciousness by which even the physical light is visible. The sun, the moon and the stars borrow their light from Prakash. Without this light of consciousness, nothing can appear. Consciousness is the Supreme Light or Prakash. Wherever there is an appearance of any object or form, there is light, and wherever there is light, there is consciousness.Therefore, everything appears in the light of consciousness.

Prakash is the Eternal Light without which nothing can appear. Prakash is Shiva.

Shiva is aware of His powers. This awareness of Shiva of His own power and grandeur is Vimarsh. His many powers are His Shaktis. Shakti means power. Without Shakti, Shiva would be powerless and inert. The manifestation, maintenance and reabsorption of the universe is just a play of Shiva's Shakti.

We, as individual beings, are identical with Shiva and are also of the nature of Pure Consciousness, but in a contracted form due to Shiva's Maya-Shakti. Just as the entire universe exists in Shiva, it exists in us too, but in a contracted form, just as a tree exists in a seed. In its contracted form, the individual consciousness is called *Chitta*. Therefore, there is nothing that is not Shiva. All that is, is Shiva and Shiva is Pure Consciousness.

The individual rises from *Chitta* to *Chit* in stages. When the individual soul experiences Chit or Pure Consciousness, he *realizes* that he is indeed identical with Shiva. This is the final and ultimate destiny of all individual souls. This experience is necessary because only with experience we can understand the True nature of the Self. On realizing the Self as Chit, the individual attains mukti or liberation.

Moksha or liberation is nothing but the awareness of one's True nature.

Various means and methods that lead to the ultimate goal were revealed to the saints by Lord Shiva Himself. These means and methods are described in detail in scriptures like Shiva Sutras and Vijnana Bhairava.

So, we see that all that is, is Shiva. Shiva is Pure unbounded Consciousness. This consciousness cannot be divided. The entire universe exists in this mass of consciousness. All that exists, exists within the range of consciousness. Lord Shiva is the immanent and transcendent Reality. He pervades all. Even matter is frozen Cosmic

Consciousness. It flows freely and unobstructed, pervading all. Shiva is the life of our life.

Our inner Self is of the nature of *Satchidananda* - Sat (Truth), Chit (Pure Consciousness) and Ananda (Bliss). That is what is meant by the mantra *'Shivoham Shivoham Satchidanandoham'*. I am Shiva of the nature of Pure Consciousness and Bliss.

Imagine an infinite string or thread that runs through a million gems keeping them all together forming one garland. The entire cosmos can be compared to that garland; we are the individual gems and the thread is pure consciousness that flows through our inner core and sustains the entire cosmos/garland. However, this pure consciousness is not just within, it is also outside of us. The entire universe is floating in consciousness. And the entire universe is made of the stuff of consciousness itself. So, we see that everything is indeed consciousness.

The yogi aims to merge with this universal consciousness. That is complete Self-God Realization.

When a yogi merges with this infinite consciousness, he identifies himself with this consciousness. And because this consciousness is everything there is to be. The yogi declares, *"I Am Everything! I Am the Universe!"*

This realization comes in stages. These stages are well explained in Kashmir Shaivism.

Such yogis are venerated as Shiva Himself. They may or may not receive supernatural powers. Even when they do, they do not reveal or use those powers because they do not want to interfere with the natural laws of the universe.

Chapter Eight

The Relation Between Man and the Supreme Spirit

***

The Supreme Spirit which is pure infinite consciousness and light, shines and radiates. The sparks emanating from this Supreme Spirit are the *jivatmas* or souls that are also of the nature of pure consciousness and light. At this level, there is no difference between the Supreme and the Soul.

As the dream world of a sleeping man is nothing but a play of the subconscious mind of the dreamer. The world is nothing but a play of the mind of the Cosmic Creator. He Himself assumes many forms and accepts limitations so that the play goes on. However, He Himself remains detached and unaffected as a Silent Witness.

The individual souls are wrapped in a fine causal body made of pure consciousness and light, which in turn is wrapped in a subtle body of energy and mind called the astral body, which is then wrapped in the gross physical body fit for the physical world of matter. As the consciousness descends from causal to subtle to gross, the soul forgets its true identity and gets lost in the world of forms. However, like in any other play, when the player gets bored and tired in the end, realizes that it's only a play and nothing real; a soul tired of its worldly existence starts searching for Truth. The Truth is then revealed to such a yearning soul and it ascends back to its Source and realizes that there is no difference between the Soul and the Supreme. They are essentially one and the same. The Supreme alone is the soul of all beings. Thus, ends the play for this soul as it realizes itself. Such a soul is then liberated from the world and rests in its Source for eternity.

The goal of every individual inhabiting this world, whether he knows it or not is to realize this unity or oneness between man and Spirit. This is only possible through Self-effort. We must use our free will to attain this goal and not become slaves of sense-pleasures and this world of forms as everything here is temporary.

Sorrow, pain and suffering are only a part of this physical world. They are the effects of wrong actions of the past performed by individuals living in ignorance. Therefore, the knowledge of Truth or Divine Wisdom alone can lead one from this world of ignorance to the world of light.

Chapter Nine

Our World – Real or Unreal?

***

Some say the world is real, while some call it unreal. According to the scriptures (Upanishads), all that is temporary and transitory is unreal and all that is permanent, and eternal is Real.

The world is both real and unreal. It is real because it is essentially Consciousness itself and Consciousness is real. And it is unreal because it does not have an independent existence apart from Consciousness.

Since the world is Consciousness itself, Consciousness alone exists. Consciousness alone is real and anything apart from it cannot exist. And if we see anything as apart from Consciousness or the Supreme, it is only due to ignorance. So, we can say that the world exists as Consciousness and does not exist as the world.

When a Yogi experiences this Cosmic Consciousness, the world disappears for Him for as long as He remains in that transcendental state where his mind is put to rest. In that state, the yogi experiences his true nature. He realizes his soul nature and experiences pure bliss, peace, and infinity. He realizes that he is indeed one with the Supreme Cosmic Consciousness. He is fully aware in that state but is formless. This world of name and form disappears and awareness alone reigns.

The moment the mind is activated, and thoughts begin to arise, the world appears again.

Chapter Ten

The Nature of the Self

***

The Self is nothing but pure consciousness itself. However, it is called 'Self' because it can be experienced directly within one's own self. And when thus realized, the individual does not identify with his body or material possessions but with the Self that is pure consciousness and immanent and transcendent. He sees unity in the apparent diversity. The Self is the soul of all beings, called as Atma in Hinduism. In common terms, Atma refers to individual jivas or souls and

Paramatma refers to the Supreme Soul.

Some describe it as void because it is empty, but it is not void because this emptiness is not nothingness though it seems to be so. It is Consciousness and therefore, it cannot be nothing or empty or void.

Even though it sits within the hearts of all, men living in ordinary consciousness do not directly experience it because it is beyond the reach of mind and senses. Therefore, all sorrow we see in this world only belongs to the mind and body. The Self is untouched by it.

The Self is undivided. It is One Being that reflects in the infinite beings, giving them life and energy. Therefore, though one, it appears as many. The 'Self' in you is the same 'Self' in me. Therefore, you and I are One. When the Self is realized through direct experience, all notions of division and separation are given up.

When one perceives oneself as separate from others, there is ignorance because this kind of notion only arises when the individual is identifying himself with his body. Even as the million rays of the sun are nothing but sun and there is only one sun, we are all nothing but Self and there is only one Self.

The Self is established in every atom of existence, yet it does not move even while these atoms are constantly moving. The space in the pot does not move when the pot is moved. And yet the pot is contained in space itself. Similarly, the Self does not move as everything is contained in the Self itself.

The Self is pure intelligence through which nature sustains itself.

Anything that is perceived as apart from this supreme cosmic consciousness is due to the delusion of the individual mind which is still experiencing its limited individual consciousness. When this mind is emptied of the mind-stuff, one experiences Super consciousness.

Those who have experienced the Self (pure consciousness) know this to be True.

Those who have not yet realized the Self fail to see the unity in diversity due to Maya. Through the practice of yoga*, when the mind is made calm, one ascends and transcends this delusive state and becomes One with the One.

Chapter Eleven

The Root Cause of Bondage

✳✳✳

What is bondage?

A French priest, Pierre Teilhard de Chardin, beautifully explained, *"We are not human beings having a spiritual experience. We are spiritual beings having a human experience."*

We are spiritual beings. We are the soul, the Self. We have unlimited potentialities and powers. We are a spark of the Supreme Light. Thus, we are Light! This Supreme Light caught up in the human body, and oblivion to its own essential nature and Truth is bondage.

The Roost cause of bondage is ignorance (*avidya*) and desires for worldly objects. Ignorance can only be destroyed by Knowledge of the Self. The Self is devoid of desire.

One who possesses a real diamond does not crave for fake ones. Similarly, one who has found the Self, does not crave for worldly objects.

The belief that we are not the Supreme Spirit, but individual beings separate from God and each other leads to bondage. Affirming the Truth, that we are One with the Supreme Spirit, that we are Pure Consciousness and that we are all one, leads to liberation.

Chapter Twelve

The Role and Importance of a Guru

***

"Guru stands for Reality, for Truth, for what is. He is a realist in the highest sense of the term. He cannot and shall not come to terms with the mind and its delusions. He comes to take you to the Real; don't expect him to do anything else."

~ Nisargadutta Maharaj

"Meeting with a great soul is hard to obtain, and never fails to save the

soul.

Through the mercy of God we get such Gurus. There is no difference between Him and His (own) ones. Seek, therefore, for this."

~ Narada Bhakti Sutras

Many people, especially in the west, wonder why we need a Guru.

An American man once asked me, "It's between me and God. Why do I need a Guru?"

I asked him, "Why do we send our children to school? Why do we need teachers? Why can't our children study on their own?"

I continued, "A Guru is a teacher. Just like we have science teachers, math teachers, history teachers, we have spiritual teachers. Just like we have science and history textbooks, we have scriptures. But do we ask our children to study from the textbooks on their own and pass the tests? No! We need teachers to simplify the complex concepts and present them in a simple and fun way which can be easily understood by children. For the same reason, we need Spiritual teachers.

Just like we have 'Bachelor of Education' and similar degrees that validate people's teaching licenses, his/her own Self-Realization is the teaching license for a Spiritual Guru.

There are an infinite number of scriptures available. It is impossible for us to study them all. A Self-Realized Guru is someone who has walked the path before you. He doesn't just teach from the scriptures, he teaches from his own experience.

If you want to eat a mango, what would be the easier way. Would it be easier to buy the seeds, sow them, nurture and take care of the trees, wait for the mangos to ripe and then pluck them and have them or would it be easier to just go to the market and buy mangoes? Most of us would prefer the second way as it would save a lot of time and energy, with the agricultural part left to the experts.

Similarly, studying the scriptures on our own would be time consuming, confusing and in some cases distressing. The Guru will give you exactly what you need and at the right time.

Let me give you another example, when you hire a fresh college graduate, you don't make him a V.P of the company directly, do you? Why? Because you know that he lacks the necessary knowledge and experience required to become a V.P. You train him first by providing a mentor. He undergoes rigorous training and works hard for many years. He gathers knowledge and experience slowly. Finally, after many years of dedication to the organization, when the owner of the company is pleased with him, he may choose to promote him as a V.P. Similarly, the Guru trains you. You have to be committed to him, to God and to your own self for many years before you reach the final goal. It is a long journey.

A Guru does not stand between you and God. He is the bridge between you and God."

The source of bondage is 'avidya' or ignorance. As long as there is ignorance, we are subject to rebirth. Due to this ignorance, we do not see the light of God that shines within us. The word 'Guru' means 'Dispeller of Darkness'. A Guru leads us from darkness to light, from ignorance to divine wisdom, from bondage to liberation (moksha).

In India, we say, "Guru is God!" Because a Guru is someone who has merged his individual consciousness with God's Supreme Consciousness. Devotees serve the Guru because they know that by serving the guru, they are serving the Lord.